Fierce Geometry

Poems

Mary Brancaccio

Get Fresh Publishing, A Non-Profit Corp.
PO Box 901,
Union, NJ 07083

www.gfbpublishing.org

ISBN: 979-8-2180632-2-1

Library of Congress Control Number: 2022945471

Cover design & layout: Donovan Crumpton
Cover Image / Photograph: "Badwater Basin, Death Valley" by Madeleine Brancaccio

typesetting/design:
culture glut llc
cultureglut.com

This book was typeset in Adobe Garamond Pro.

To my mother, Deanna Mae D'Andrea Fortkort

Table of Contents

I.   Children's Park By London's Imperial

War Museum..3

Budding...4

For Cosmo, Shooter of Pigeons............................6

Dirt and Rust...8

Zankat America...10

On the Road from Oukaimeden...........................12

Tao of Our Breakup...14

Corset Dream...15

What I Lost; What I Gather................................16

I Discover Geometry.......................................18

David's Room...20

Bliss is an Odd Remembrance for Such a

Wormwood Day...21

II.   The Cancer of Never Letting Go........................25

Because Mom Always Gets the Last Word................50

III.   Idling...55

Tea with Ann...56

After Ann Tweets of Her Father's Death..................58

Loma Prieta Quake, 1989.................................60

Kaisertown: A Tragedy in Five Acts.......................62

I Dream Wanda Plays Me Chopin.........................70

Forgiveness...72

Mistress of Buttons & Keys................................74

To the Woman on the Eastbound Midtown Direct.........75

On the Verge...76

Slow Journeying in the West..............................78

Birthing Pigs in Kingman, Arizona........................79

Acknowledgments..81

Notes...83

I.

Children's Park by London's
Imperial War Museum

Like a widow outside a circle of wives, I watch my son play
as the other mothers, who've grown old together in tower flats,
eye me. One brings me tea in a chipped cup

from the mother shack, and we talk, though my accent breaks
as discordant notes on her Cockney ear. She carries my news
back to her crow-eyed fold. I am a mystery queried a moment:

a daguerreotype of a dead aunt in her Sunday best
a bronze visage on a foreign coin, too far removed
from the day's laundry piles and thin soup to matter much.

Chill of October surprises with its sudden arrival outside
this mausoleum to empire that jails bedlam under brocade
and hushed paint. Near its iron gate, a last rose

holds its own against the onrush, so I press my face to it,
hear grandma's song, sweet with its honey of lullaby, here
in this country she loved and despised, its queen, its reach

that clawed its way into her mother's house to claim
a son. I am a child that suckled at the breast
of resentment. Some here would pen the likes of me

in wired camps, death traps, workhouses for the poor
another stolen generation. But I walk these streets free,
my boy in my arms, knowing our suitcase lives

will not end in this grey whale that swallowed a world
and then spit out what it could not consume.

Budding

We three girls squeeze in on benches
to play poker. Across from me is the boy
I don't know but want to. Alice's father
slides beside me. His thigh rubs mine.
His stare. His nudge of knee beneath
the kitchen table. Too close.
His gaze burns my cheeks.

Next morning, I stand in the spring creek
teeth clattering, purpled toes curled
in torn sneakers, threads bent
like eelgrass. Ribbons of light distort
arms and legs, rocks and drowned
leaves. I circle a minnow in dappled light
in a stream fenced by concertina wire
swollen with rain. He watches on the bank
and drinks beers with my dad.

When I ride back to the cabin, heat radiates
off the black mare's back, warms my limbs.
I cling to his daughter to steady myself.
Horsehair crosshatches my thighs.

Before the boys and men arrive
I jerk the water pump up
down up down quick quick
till silver gushes from its spout.
I rinse away my noticing
and being noticed.

Girltalk at night as we slip toward sleep
three across a double bed. I conjure
that boy with downy lips but something crowds
like duckweed on a pond. On the brink
of this wilderness, cicadas rise to fever pitch.
Her father stares from the hall as we curl
together. Over the ridge, a flash of lightning.
A growl like thunder deep inside me.

For Cosmo, Shooter of Pigeons

As a child, I dreamed of *heavenly hosts*
As bright stars, disembodied heads, their eyes
Dark as mirrors, makers of godlike praise
All lips and wings — nothing like my body
With appetites, angers — a Milky Way:
Clouds of song soaring in unified verse.

But what's their choral refrain, what's their verse?
Do they sing of dying street trees, of hosts
Of locusts descending on fields, the way
Weed's structure rivals orchid's beauty, eyes
Of the beholder mere carbon body?
Glory to unraveling, sing its praise.

What of Cosmo, as plain as a thumb, praise
Be his pale face, his pimpled skin, give verse
With celestial tongue to his body.
See now his loud triumphant blasts, you hosts,
As he shoots pigeons off the church's dome, eyes
Glazed and focused, never seeing the way

Ahead, the death that awaits him, the way
One dies and another is saved, let praise
Ring from the rafters. Let us open eyes
And throats, let all creation join the verse
Until we form cacophony. Oh hosts
Adoring the weakness of the body,

See desire convulse his mortal body.
Let us understand when we look his way
His magnificence, a face among hosts
Of heavenly choirs lighting the sky, praise
Be his shuffling into manhood, the verse
Of the streets on his lips, pain in his eyes.

No, don't look away, transfix on his eyes,
Ticking bomb of cancer in his body,
A brace of dead birds at his feet, verse
And chapter, nicotine air that made way
Into his lungs, staking the path for praise
Over his casket, beneath painted hosts

Of winged cherubs inside the dome, a way
To give thanks to his Almighty, to praise
Dying over plates of communion hosts.

Dirt and Rust

On that rutted road through the Midi-Atlas, I fell hard
for Mohamed's deserts. First startled by absence of trees

and vast nothingness, I learned to spot the flowers in the dust.
Bitter tang rose from camel turds glistening with grass.

Road apples. I made him laugh when I called them that.
Our last trip together was his final gift. Even now, as I travel

America's west, I compare his world and mine. Once,
in Death Valley, at an old ghost town, I searched for remnants:

rusted nails, cans hammered flat for shingles. I dreamt
the storm song on a miner's tin roof as he lay awake,

thoughts of the woman he'd send for when he'd panned
his fortune from dirt. In the hills, wide alluvial fans mapped

gathered destinies during rare rains, congruent
paths, what he and I would never have, our lives

touching for some years, like palm lines of life and heart
that blend before diverging. He'd ask, *What does it mean,*

hick. You're a real hick? Without translation, histories are lost.
When the plane arrived without him, I stood for hours

under the dogwoods, afraid to move, flooded with longing
so deep, I was sure I'd drown. I tried to remember our last

phone call, over that faint line from Rabat: his hope for a visa,
his wait for an interview. When Fatima hennaed my hands,

he sat between us, to interpret. It took three hours.
She traced each painted line with melted wax. To pass the time,

she shared the story of her life: her husband in America,
who took a new wife and left her waiting. All the years spent

praying to Allah, imploring fakirs. She read my future in red clay.
On my left palm, a rose. On the right, a brilliant red comet.

Zankat Amerika

Here in Rabat
trash tumbles down
a gutted cliff
by the Atlantic
on a dead-end
street named
for my country.

Picking her
way down mounds
in a floral hijab she
plucks out a plastic jug.
Her man probes debris
with twin magnets on a stick
filling his bag
with bottle caps
and a glass flask.
Bit by bit, they tease
what of utility
survives. Below
an ocean's restless waves
startle seagulls —
their orchestral screeches
like dry bows across
taut strings.

Deep in me beats
a ragpicker's pulse
gathering, gathering.
A horde memory:
each frame
of my lost film
a button saved
in a mason jar.
Ancestral fear
of hard times.
So I dig
debris to discover
what I lack
on my own Avenue
of the Americas
where yesterday's garbage
may be salvaged
for free, if pride
is not an obstacle.

On the Road from Oukaimeden

A man stood in the icy lane
to warn us of a stalled truck

at the bend in the road. The wind,
like a lover, kissed the hem of his blue

djellabah. The car's hood swung
like a second hand, back tire churning

gravel as you braked to avoid the man,
the truck, the rim of the road. You threw

your arm across me. We flew forward,
then stopped. The truck's crumpled edge

bracketed one valley edge. We both sucked in
breath. Before us, a bleak abyss.

The car motor purred. Stillness, and the giddy spin
of tire on open air. Across the valley, a new bride

in red robes goaded her flock of sheep
through a cleft in the hills. A gust lifted

a fist of snow and dashed it into the air.
Distant orchards of almond trees in flower,

as if they'd caught the frost from Oukaimeden
in their green branches. The thud of my heart,

I almost lost you. Lost us. Our car rocking
gently with the gusts. The man calling out in Arabic.

Another man appearing. Then a third.
We're pulled from the precipice. After,

you joined the others to coax a nervous driver
through a hairpin curve. As you bent

your shoulder to the truck's steel frame,
I thought, we've reached the end.

You belong here. I am just your visitor.

Tao of Our Breakup

Slivers of almonds pressed to sweet dough
remind me of the half-moons in your nails,

pearly as the glint of tooth inside your smile.

And on your lips, caramel trace
of what you've savored, sugar rimming

the edge of your mouth. Your coffee's swirl an empty
dialogue box inside our cartoon romance,

our words always just beyond our grasp:
pregnant silences, knowing glances,

cigarettes burning to filterless ends
inside an ashtray from the Golden Nugget.

Viva Las Vegas. We did everything backwards:
our honeymoon closed our last chapter, we built

our table of contents from IKEA boxes,
dreamt of faraway mountains with brides

dressed in red, their caftans billowing
like absentee ballots, punch cards

full of dangling propositions.

Corset Dream

I pluck a tick from my shin, then cherry blossoms.

My ribs pry open like stuck sills, unleashing ten thousand moths,

stirred ashes, grandma's hankies, coins with wings.

I come to you loomed and wired, tattooed with sinew and vein:

beetle feet crawled my vena cava, tangled roses.

My bones, spokes from a bent wheel. Useless as that 45

tumbling through my neuron jukebox: a cowboy croons

the more I learn to care for you, the more we drift apart…

to the beat of a slammed screen door. I am tattered coat,

worn at the elbows,

loose button, unraveled cuff, warm despite the holes.

I need some thread, some needle wax, some vinyl scratch,

some salt-stained glass, some shut-eye.

My hand hennaed like a bride's waved goodbye on the tarmac,

scattered red seeds in a tub, then closed over a worry stone.

What I Lost; What I Gather

Chilly: spring water on dust-streaked feet.

Summer sky mosaic by an oak branch. *Look,*
he points to a band of thunderheads, *purple light.*

A swaying rope bridge, gaps between planks.

Oil rainbow shimmers in the creek. Near
bubbles from beneath a rock: *crawdad.*

On honeysuckle stigma: beads of nectar.

Sunlight filtered by grey barn slats
falls like splinters of hay on my brother's shirt.

Dead robin's open throat, a red ant.

Shepherd bitch, teats swollen with milk,
wanders left field between third and second base.

My hands ride a tree's gnarled bark.
The best apples always out of reach.

From a burning nest, a swarm of hornets.
My father stained with kerosene and cut grass.

Sometimes hot tar looks like elephant skin.

From the window of a Greyhound, orange scars
of eroded southern clay. In Charlottesville

I dial a number from a public phone,
a call for an ex-con on the bus,

They let him out. He's on the bus, headed home.

I Discover Geometry

I guide my carbon pencil's point
through arc and line as I birth

elegant forms on fields of graphing paper:
tessellations and dilations. I learn of love, the great

transversal that creates congruence from disparate
beings. In school, I never master complex sums,

but still I learn. Slopes and arrows flood
my dreams as my body shifts weight,

drops its ballast of gravity into my pelvis.
My breasts and hips bend lines into curves.

Startled by the fast-changing landscape,
I conjure patterns on pages, a secret

inside my delicate arches: a face
beneath mine – antipodal points

caught within spheres of attractions.
Years later, I found the man I sought. My thumb

marks the nape of his neck, my fingers navigate
scapulae of his back, his nipple's raised ridge.

My hands ride the concavity of his lower back, angles
of knees and elbows nestled together, as fluidity

open to possible worlds, damp hair pressed
against his hip. In time, our breathless gasps subside.

We fall toward sleep, embossed on wrinkled sheets.
We have weathered broken space, parallel lives of discontent,

skewed paths to learn fidelity is less a ring than a Möbius strip.
What little I knew of love's fierce geometry.

David's Room

I climb to your room nestled against rafters.
Day's heat stills the air. I enter it swimming:
that beach in Ghana where you studied
the history of conquest. Fierce
as a lover, you pored over ancient ledgers
as if to memorize each and every name.
Outside Elmina, where they crammed captives
in dank cellars, you shook, unable to enter
without hearing anguish of women children men
their terror still suspended in its salted air.

We read to one another curled naked
in bed, Simenon's three novellas
of Africa. A fevered swain
is seduced by his landlady. Her damp
dress clings to curve of belly and breast
diaphanous silk. Her dark pubic hair
carries wood smoke, orchid
curry. As he dies of dengue, he discerns
he's been duped. We revel in Simenon's
harsh world, far from this Southern city
with its docile monuments that brick in rage.

I'll leave you your welding tools, your radio,
even that book of names with its stained white cover
& blue linen seams. Those are yours. Inside your bag
a canister of used film I slip in my pocket.

Bliss is an Odd Remembrance for
Such a Wormwood Day

Orchard Lane, cabin in ruins, space for a chair,
age-yellow notebook. Inkwell brims with water fleas
lucent organs, flowers from ash, feathery limbs.

Trove on the cusp of broken, field on the brink of seed –
my home? Rain falls in torrents, sung in by crows.
Hardly a word spoken without a glint of bone.

I've gauged the width of narrows, I've gauged the weight
of a shroud. Evergreen needles above me
sew shut my dry-tongue mouth.

II.

The Cancer of Never Letting Go

Cancer was the price she paid for hoarding
what she should forget: anger and hurt.

Or so my mother claimed.

Didn't she have a right to rail against the world?

Born poor
her father's café torched by loan sharks
her mother's madness and sadism.

How my Grandma Wanda preyed
on her kids. Some of them.
The three that resembled their father:
dark eyes, dark hair, deep olive skin.

Taunting my mother faced for her given name:
Deanna D'Andrea
too many vowels, too sing-song.

Daughter of immigrants, left
in a *home* for misbegotten orphans
and war refugees

after her father left

after Wanda went mad.

#

Mom paints. I'm her model.
I learn to sit deathly still as she works:

me, in *Blonde Girl on Stoop with Puppy*
me, in lace splendor, dress and veil: *First Communion*
me, teenager buried in *Reading Mary, Queen of Scots.*
Me, in a dressing room trying on a skirt: *Are You Pregnant?*

I lied. She never painted that one.

#

Pain fractures wrinkles under her dark eyes.
Hush of oxygen between words. I can't
hold her gaze, her hair now stubble, scalp
dotted with open sores. Stench of pee.

My eye wanders

her sterile room
spotless
but for hovering dust clouds
on sprinkler heads over her bed.

Magnetized, they draw fragments
of skin, of hair
detritus of the dying.

A Milky Way of DNA.

One day, some janitor in a fit of efficiency
will sweep all of them away.

#

She naps, I fantasize.

Camera's eye pans over city street
trails a woman.

she stops to realign her stockings
under her lover's gaze.

He meets her
at the door. His lips hungry for her _____
his hand slips beneath her _____
his fingers search for taut _____

Cut. Camera rewinds.
The street.
The door.
The stop to fix her hose.

She knows: he watches.
She feels warmth of his watching

a theft of sorts.

Audible gasp for breath.

I am back in the room with the ventilator.
The street dissolves, the lover gone.

#

Nipples tilt down, dripping water
dried dugs of an old woman naked
in the shower, her belly bruised
by needle marks above sparse pubic
hair. Bald after radiation, her skull
ringed by short white stubble, buttocks
two empty saddlebags. She braces
her frail frame against the tiles
and stands: like Selket, healer of stings,
full-bellied, like all our women kin.
Dark-eyed mother, a thousand blessings.
Her lips pursed, not a kiss. Resilience.
Is it cruel to let her feel the cold?
I press towels to her mottled skin
and swaddle her as if she were my child.

#

I never asked for this justice
cruel in its humiliation.

I never asked for power to hurt
in return. My hands chop
impossible mats of her falling locks.

I pushed her away.
I learned to give
only so much of myself.

I'd store morphine in the fridge
for nights that stretched
into thin hours of darkness,
mollifying her when she asked,

Was I a good mother?

Merciless is her god.

\#

Here, in this vacant church in Buffalo, will I find
the vowels I lost? Are they hidden in hymnals?
In porcelain cool that pools over holy water?

I can't remember the next line of prayer —
I've been away –
I kneel on a splintered pew beneath a water-stained heaven
below a Madonna whose blue chador peels free of the plaster.

As a kid, I saved pennies for the poor, slid them in bronze
boxes on the wall, and then lit paraffin candles.

Now soot covers the chapel wall behind the Infant of Prague:
all of our best intentions, carbon swirls against the faded pink.

#

Night. I tiptoe
from my bed to hers.
I am…twelve? Eleven?
my flannel gown falls flat
from my shoulders.

My fingers hover
over her sleeping face
above her lips, where I reach
to feel her breath.

Are you alive?

Some nights I pull dread
around my thin body like a blanket.
Squeeze my eyes, stop up my ears
to forget her fish-flat eyes
her voice, deadpan:

One night.
You wait and see.

I'll slice my throat. My
blood, my life will drain away.

In a few seconds
it'll all be over.

Warm and red,
like a garnet necklace.

#

Note from my mother to me at ten:

When you get home from school,
wax floor with a second coat.
Peel potatoes and carrots,
start stew for dinner.

I fold each note into paper doves
and burn them so they rise:
a phoenix of sacred ash.

#

What if you can't forgive? she asks
on day five of radiation

the morning her hair falls out
like Gordian knots.

More scalp revealed beneath each snip,
as her baldness emerges.

I struggle with the scissors.
Say nothing.

She asks, *Please forgive me
I thought I would lose you.*

She morphs into a fledgling in my hands.

#

I was late from school.
I'd missed my bus. I had
no answers. I flipped
my waist-length hair.
and turned away.

I saw in her eyes: raptor.
She grabbed her scissors and cut. I ran.
She spent her rage on my locked door.

Then she cajoled.
(What's worse: anger or apology?

Or how a voice changes to manipulate?)

Later: she sheared off the rest of my hair.
so no one would know. Next day,
she picked me up at school.
Anyone ask about your haircut?

Definition of sarcasm: */Nice haircut/*

\#

We stagnated, a slime green pond
deeply rooted in tangled weeds.

We were taught to drown all:
thoughts, deeds, half-told stories.

A dock juts over clear water
but swimmers never visit

no boat breaks its glass.

#

Doctor: *The cancer is in bad places.*

In the feathered language of diagnosis
where can I land?

We wait on the night nurse
and the sleeping pill.

I should have let you study painting.
All those Saturdays scrubbing floors.
washing clothes. I never let you go.
You were the oldest. My only girl.

Did you want to be a painter? she asks.
I lie and deny. I say: *I learned so much from you*
all those weekends on my hands and knees.

One Saturday at art class in the basement
of St. James' School, I draw a sleeping fawn
for her – she hates it. Lines all off.
Color too heavy in parts.

Look, I can't afford these classes.
I need you to clean on Saturdays.

#

Two decades of chapped hands
and ammonia stinging my nostrils.
I scrubbed my brothers' excrement
off toilets. Scoured scuff marks
from her kitchen floor.

I say: *You taught me never to fear
hard work.*

Instructions to
the Daughter:
How to Wash a Floor.

Don't ever use a mop.
Do it on your knees.

Today, my shoulders ache.
I have forgotten the feel of fresh sheets.
Dust pools in corners of steps.
Film falls on stacks of books.

I give up.

Hope weighs too much.

#

Love is a narrow bed.

Clatter of shutters. Whistle
as wires harp our house.

Air bleeds around a loose door
and window cracks.

Another storm surge:

rattle of panes, flicker of lights.
The lamp blinks twice and dies.

Don't go.
I can't face it alone:

blackness, rising water.

#

Blood weeps
from needle pricks

across her bruised belly.
I dab drops with a tissue.

Thirsty, it drinks.

I crumple it, drop it
in the toilet.

It undulates: wings
against a porcelain sky

brilliant red feathers.

#

She drifts toward sleep, then suddenly grabs my hand.

Do it. Create. Let the rest go.
Who in the hell remembers
if you kept a clean house?

But what peace in a clean house!

Each sock rolled in its drawer
each plate stacked in the cupboard
each book in its place, its spine

supported by its kin.

\#

I rub salve into her cracked
and bleeding feet, to keep her mind

after morphine fails, to stave off pain
that seizes her like contractions, as if death

is a kind of birth. Perhaps the soul swells
and bursts the saline waters that hold it,

as her lips pull back from her gritted teeth
to unleash groans. What breaks us in the end —

distance, despair, fatigue — travels thin solder
of nerves that twine fissures, quick pulses

of electrical charge, as if filament
inside a bulb suddenly flashes

blue jolts, slows
and then burns itself out.

#

This child asks for resurrection.

This child asks
      for flicker of eyelid,
          for finger's twitch,
              for the rise and fall of her mother's chest.

As if the soul as hand
      could return
          to animate
              the glove of the body.

This child asks —

    #

But a grown girl mired in sorrow
says, it's done. It's all over.

Soon they will come for her mother's body.

All that remains are cold things:
        an empty bed
        a plastic sheet
        rust on the rim of an oxygen tank.

      #

Once there was fire.
Now only ashes, spent fury.

What mattered once is now
a burden. Cold things:

glass.
pewter.
marble.

#

Why was I never enough? Why did it please you
to punish me? I learned to thwart you in silence,
hide my rebellions, though they lingered
like cigarette smoke in my clothes. I ran
to the other side of the continent to be freed
of your efforts to sculpt me into what I could never be.
Seared in my mind are your acts of cruelty, yet you always
found something in me to love. Your conditions for approval
were a heavy yoke. The world you wanted
is not the world I want. You stuck fast to rules
and saw small transgressions as sparks
to extinguish. When I feel the fire in me,
I think of you, all anger and flame. I wanted your faith,
your insistence on a just God who would level
the injustices of this world. But yours was god
as weapon, not God as love.

#

As they lift her casket into the hearse
her daughter wails: *Don't go, don't go, don't go.*

I am watching myself as a swimmer drowning in the distance.

#

after:
sickening scent of lilies
bare bulb in a hallway late at night
dry cleaner bags over tea dresses
crumpled tissues pressed into pockets of all her old clothes
enormous pot for spaghetti
mouse shit in drawer with kitchen knives
pink prom shoes, a rifle
acrid taste of grapefruit in the morning
clocks that blink zeroes to mark the brownout
porch lantern filled with rain
and on her bedroom wall, an icon of the black madonna

#

If there is darkness, give me light:

arms wrapped around love's body
like a child whose anger breaks

against an ancient breast.

I ask of the goddess
of small things:

listen to my prayers.

#

Because Mom Always Gets the Last Word

The moment I birthed you, I knew you'd leave.
When you failed to thrive on my milk,
I knew I would never be enough. And yet,
you opened my world in a way I never expected.

I hungered for the feeling you gave me, the pure
love of you: my own child, mine and mine alone.
It fed me for years. And then when the others came,
I could see in your face the shadow of my betrayal.

I still loved you, though someone else was in my arms.
Mother love is as elastic as a womb, expanding to fit more inside.
I understand you might not see it this way —
you who so flourished in my care those early years,
becoming my sun and my moon. I loved you so,

I feared I would break you. One morning I set you
high on the slide and I ran to the bottom to catch you,
only to watch in horror as you stood up and walked
off the top, falling face first into the sand below.
I have broken her, I told the doctor. He laughed,
knowing the resilience of young bodies better than I.

But as you grew into your own, I became afraid
of your leaving and your wild side. So much like
my mother. I feared what I had unleashed
on the world. I fought to curb your defiance, what
leads women to dereliction and insanity. I curbed
the same impulse in myself through hard work
and prayer, the stays that make a woman honest.

You would not become your grandmother, of this
I was sure. Call what I did cruel, but look
what I made of you: forthright and compassionate,
the woman I so wanted you to be, the girl
of chances and power. My control left
the cold taste of the bit in your mouth.
In the end, you left me long before I left you.

III.

Idling

Blossoming from the crumbling remains
of Petey, our dead family cat
an overpowering stench
neighbors blamed on the gingko —

inside his ribs, pennies fell into wells
as our daughters wished for his return.
Deep in the green copper of words
are missives I wrote, but never sent.

Carload of kids, you in the driver's seat
tie askew, wearing that look I dread.
Snap to synapse, the gap
between neurons, the miracle of us:

How it keeps. How it keeps.

Tea with Ann

I don't know when we started our habit
of long talks over pots of tea

or why it felt so familiar.

And I wonder if we'd been born
elsewhere, would we have met

in a post office line, or waiting

for a bus, instead of
in the cafeteria

at Bishop O'Connell

sophomore year?
I was the one eating alone

when you came along.

But is seems as if
I can't imagine growing old

without you.

Who else will laugh
at *the point of no return*

from the priest's lecture on loss
of virginity, played on a tinny cassette

to a classroom of horny sixteen
year-olds, all bucking to lose it

by graduation? I still can't pass
that donut shop in Vienna

without feeling queasy over crème puffs

after you and I got high and you taught me
how crème-filled donuts were made.

And didn't we talk the dawn in
over mothers and lovers,

the ones we lost, the ones we buried.
Only you understand the gap that grew

between ourselves and our brothers,
after our mothers died.

And the aging fathers we loved,
god, how they wore us down.

I promise this summer, no really,
I'll help you tame your back lot.

The kids and I will be over.

I'll bring a rake and pruning shears.
You'll put on a pot of tea.

After Ann Tweets of Her Father's Death

In the middle of Union Station
loud track announcements
glitterati of donut stands
and coffee-to-go, I find myself
drowning, a girl in a pink bikini
in a black-bottomed pond.
It's June and my twelfth
birthday and I almost die, water
fills my lungs, only they are not
mine but my son's, he chokes
newly born, air strange in his wet
lungs, but it's your father who's died
lungs flooded with fluids
as my great-grandfather
chokes on his own bad lungs
and passes my mother his
bloodied kerchief. She coughs
and passes it to my uncle
as I hold a hand against a broken
rib to stop the stabbing pain
when I cough from pneumonia
after I totaled my car in a frozen swamp
but my aunt picks up a brush, traces
across my sky the arc of her surgical
scar: instructions on how to dissect
a body, for poor children with weak
lungs and bad habits, but I digress.

Let me wind back to the leap
from death to birth, an old man
in his hospice bed, you my beloved Ann,
the daughter crying at his side, because
like me, you resist the linear nature of time.
But isn't life a conga line in a hostile
universe that always ends
with a broken refrain? La de da.

Loma Prieta Quake, 1989

I reach toward a cantaloupe
and tremors begin. Shocked
by my weightless arms
I whisper, *Where's the baby?*

The floor undulates
beneath my feet. Pinned
to a pillar, a store clerk pleads
Oh god, oh god, oh god.

Yesterday, at Children's Hospital
David and I sat in a hall, fingers woven
with worry, our baby's skin
bright copper. Forced to stop

nursing, my breasts engorged
and our freezer filled with my milk.
We imagined our TV campaign:
begging strangers for money

for baby Nicky's transplant. Now
I silence sound as glass cracks,
ceiling tiles creak and snap,
the three of us nestled like Russian dolls.

Later, we will drive through Oakland
past the Cypress, our old route home
its snapped and twisted steel bones
its pancaked decks, its spray-painted rubble:

DOA and an arrow
Body 2nd Car

and only occasionally the word *alive*.

Kaisertown: A Tragedy in Five Acts

Act 1

Ghost girl hops and skips from kitchen to stoop,
past lots littered with glass like hosannas
to the King of Beers. She skips off broken
curbs to sidewalks uprooted by oak trees

planted by public works, then left to die.
She scuttles past the witches' haunted hut,
cut firewood stacked against their warping walls.
She skirts a corner, then leaps a chain-link fence,

steals across Big Joe's yard, where her cousin
laughs as he stands in one leg of Joe's pants
and holds out the waistband. *Look! Room for two!*
She ducks beneath a clothes line, walks the block

past Casimir's church, its doors now stripped
of copper plating by tweaking vandals.
She enters a corner bar with a brass plaque:
years he served in Korea, and her uncle's name.

Act 2

Ghost girl conjures her cousin, and the two,
cast from the warmth of a mother's kitchen,
plunge through snow to the dark park across
from Saint Casimir's, sent on an errand
to buy milk. Machines huddle on corners
in these urban streets without Sunday stores.
They take off damp gloves, feed quarters to slots.
A short hum, then cartons of milk trundle
down the chute. They talk of love. *Na pewno.*

The boy is always in love with the same
girl. Their lives fall into tandem steps, one
just ahead, and then the other catches up,
their boots pressing paths in drifts of dry snow.
They carry milk quarts back to the kitchen.
Steam from boiled kielbasa fogs the windows,
mothers halt their gossip, look at their ghost
children, pale with flushed cheeks, their eyes teared
by lake-blown wind. *What took you so long?*

Years pass. The ghost boy grows into a man
and works as an arc welder in one shop,
and then another, braves the layoffs and strikes,
wonders in awe at what a team of men
can forge from metal and fire. Then a stroke
freezes his left arm, and his work is done.

After a family wedding, where he saw
his ghost cousin, he starts to drive at night,
looking for milk machines. He uncurls bent
fingers on his left hand to steer the wheel
and drives down street after street looking for one.
Gone. Obsolete in a 24/7 world.

The next summer, ghost girl swims a lake
in the Adirondacks, her arm tracing an arc
across the summer sky, light falling in wet
drops from her fingertips as her left shoulder
rolls into a backstroke. She is panged
by remembrance: *this move is lost to him.*

Act 3

Cynthia pours a coffee and lights a Camel.
She smells it: antiseptic from a surgeon's hands
and the burnt whiff of hacksaw on cranial bone.

In the shed behind the house, ghost boy passes
ghost girl a joint, and they talk of JFK. Doubt
and conspiracy billow around them like clouds.

How will we make our lives matter? They wonder.
Returning to the kitchen, ghost girl finds her.
Auntie? What's the matter? Auntie, are you there?

She waves her hands over Cynthia's glazed eyes.
In the closet: her uncle's empty coat. After years,
of night shifts, he left his job, and never returned.

Act 4

Ghost girl doesn't know this street, its houses half-shuttered
with cheap aluminum shades, their siding matched
to one of five colors of surrender, backyards paved
black with asphalt, as if they might forget that
Great Grandma slaughtered chickens there.

She doesn't know this neighborhood, houses
maybe three hopscotch squares apart,
screens thick with soot from factory
smoke or tire fires in abandoned lots
that cover all the cars with greasy dust.

The girl can't say she recognizes the truck, its lights
on in midday, its door ajar, though her cousin
stays in place behind the wheel, as if deaf
to the cops' constant calls to *Step out of the vehicle, sir.*

Ghost girl doesn't recall the name of the videographer
hiding behind a dying bush along the north
flank of his house, where rust pockmarks
a drainpipe and a Ford with a bent side-mirror
assaults the curb. If that's her cousin in the truck,

she's not sure. Is he the same little boy
who once clung to the rubber backyard pool,
afraid to plunge into the deep, as ghost girl
splashed with his sisters that August night
under a yellow floodlight?

His thin voice is familiar, his cry too,
as his body retracts from blue shock
and he tumbles onto the road
while the cops follow protocol
for using force on recalcitrants.

She wants to know and not know
this man. To remember a sweeter time
when there was a chance he'd outgrow
his swagger, his taste for beer, his anger
fermenting inside, like a bad liver.

She wants to forgive him. He found Wanda
dead on the floor of her kitchen, two days after
a stroke cut her down while standing by the sink
to fill a kettle for morning tea. Poor Grandma.
And he drove his dad to the hospital as blood

clotted a lung, killing him two months into
retirement after decades walking a postal route,
after years of postponed surgeries to fix
his mangled knee. How he held his father's
hand and begged him to not slip away.

Maybe she should forgive him the grief
he caused his mother, her smother love
that kept him a boy in her house at forty-five,
his first time away that stint in jail for his third
DUI, caught while driving a township truck.

Dan's voice is otherworldly, skinny
as the whine of a bitter Mickey Mouse,
as he sprawls on the pavement, subdued.
Anger is the leash that keeps him down,
pain, an abstract shape on his life's canvas.
Ghost girl closes the screen and logs off.
As if she can.

Act 5

Ghost girl went North for her tenth summer.
Her auntie positioned ghost girl's brush: *Look
with the eye, sketch what you see.*

You're too thin, she fussed, so she fried
Moon Over Miami, its ochre yolks ascendant
in a sky of red bologna and seared toast.

She overlooks ghost girl's chewed nails,
her calluses that cushion her pen when she writes,
teeth marks on her fingers, sucked for comfort.
Clouds on her nail beds? Cynthia tallied:
You have seven secret lovers! she reveals.

Like her sable brushes, her auntie's fingertips
splayed and flirted as they plait braids
and flitted between canvas and stove.

In a cabana at the lake, ghost girl spied her auntie's surgical scar.
she longed to soothe its jagged edge. Decades later,
Cynthia will die alone: B-movie on TV, last cigarette

smoldered to ash in her fingers, her fridge nearly bare:
one egg, a slice of bread, a dried salami curl.
Everywhere paintings. Her auntie's last work: shirt soaked red

as if scalpel sliced from breastbone to scapula
to expose rosebuds, tightly furled.

I Dream Wanda Plays Me Chopin

Lento

(If only I had learned to play
like her) I'd move faster.
Time is all
I have and still her slips
like hemp rope
tug into a knot, her
[empty]self.

Allegretto

In the back seat
of a rusted rambler, I ride
past the asylum
outside some small town.
Too stupid not to, I ask, for I am still a child
[because the air is fresh, because, because].
I dream inside: those green empty halls
her room of peeled paint
her trash can brined with paper
choked with notes (where
are her people) engraved. An unmarked
knoll, its leaf blessed tree, her shroud
that crowded ward behind wired glass
her suffocation like
caught fish, gills fanning
bubbles on her lips
gulping, her gulp
its foam, her loam.

Andantino

A wagon idles, two men
(white coats?) one
on either side: how tight
their grasp is. I can't see —
do they leave marks? Look
at her crazy hands, look at all those
flats and sharps!

I search her song's half-notes
search for her in measures, but
never find her. All those
chords all those scales all those
trying turns:
all her gifts.

Moderato

In chains
in bed straps, in tethered wire
in shock, in cranial drill
in pills in pills in pills
wall, hairline
crack, fracture
suture, tincture for her
no cure no cure no
cure expect

sepulcher holy
holey, her hole, her whole.

Forgiveness

Here in the dark,

                         light slithers across canvas, pours

from wall to floor

Words flood my thoughts   and leap

            but fail

to coalesce.   Give us forgiveness: a definition

or what it was like, after.   I cannot write: too raw, too raw

           wound, a tomb

where my Lazarus tongue slept until wakened   in love

and words became flesh

           our bodies, clasped

as I surrender my hand

               though I held all the cards

a spatter of red across a field of morning gold

           my sheets white flags:
I surrender I surrender I surrender

        how many times can a body surrender

and is it love
is it love?

         and last, will it:

            last last last.

My door opens, my vault

          unguarded.

Mistress of Buttons & Keys

She clutches a broken jar spilling lost buttons. Look at her
wares: off an old school blazer, a brass-embossed crest
with its motto, *Excelsior!* Better a button of clamshell or *Bakelite.*

It carries no grace, but moves through holes
with the genius of calendars. Ask about that jangle
of keys at her waist. Which one sets her free?
Look, her brow darkens.

Mirror: me, a girl with a needle in one hand, a pen
in the other. These tools cut to the quick.
Give me a fresh-cut log, I'll show you
what grows on dead wood. Charm is a fungus,
it eats at the heart. Mother soil? I can attest to its iron.

Ask my mom what she fears in the blood she spies
on her young daughter's panties. Turn the tap,
and the water's too cold or too hot. It won't launder
stains. Let me not dither over tiles & tubs.
Lather is lovely but fleeting.

To the Woman on the Eastbound Midtown Direct

The scent of your pear, with its nectar, its August light,
conjured my mother at *True Value* in Shallotte
as she chatted up the man with the bumper crop.
Right off, she bought two-dozen jars, pectin,

and drove to his farm in her Caddie to pick fruit.
Like a biblical Ruth gleaning scythe-cut fields,
she gathered a trunk load of the fallen, not the split-skin
orbs, but the ripened ones sleeping in wet grass.

That Christmas, Mom gifted us jars of pear jam.
I wrapped mine in diapers when I flew to London
where the taste of summer cracked the frost grip
of winter's deprivations in my bone-cold flat.

Today, I thank you for your pear, for your ready gratitude
how you cupped it in your hands and ate deeply to its core.

On the Verge

Dozens ride in trucks to the landfill everyday.
Others, under glass, are dead souls

sealed by taxidermy. The master strings waist beads
of frog-eyed stones to entrap his beloved.   What a hungry beak.

Belly on belly, so many chords bind his love to hymns.
Crushed beneath wheels, bulbs emit hectares of song:

they light town squares with gasps, muted by broom sweeps
of weary matrons who pocket their tunes.

He is a sheller of peas on her porch of desire.
Because

I love you outlasts body's touch,

fog's absence from a mirror is no proof of death.

Never is a fork in a road through Blue Mountains.

Deer are ghost lovers crossing the meadow of her body.

Spider silk veils a face.

His tread devours a cricket.

Across the road's shoulder, legs of a doe

    broken & angled like cello bows

        teem with flies trilling between treble & clef.

Slow Journeying in the West

I-10 between Mesa and L.A.,
all wind-whipped, sunburnt rock.
Radio static between landmarks
that entrance to listening where scraps
of words, of musical notes, of phrasings
gather in the mind, then are tossed aside — *moon dog*
swamp scold, cucumber thread — beads discarded
in mind's relentless pattern search.

If the moon rises now, it fails
to illuminate. Better to have silver mica
tweet its existence to a bored
minor star. Under the earth, what sleeps
through daylight edges toward wakening, roused
by belly and bladder. Sweet dusk draws
night's shroud over my eyes. Fog descends
and moistens the cacti. Now slow ebb of breath
as if my last. With it, tired day and all its bungled tasks.

Birthing Pigs in Kingman, Arizona
for M. N.

Birth, such grunting madness: sow charges
across her pen, red-eyed. All hooves and dirt.
Blood and urine slosh into mud
beneath her trampling feet, so we dash
to rescue each newborn as it drops.

Here's the runt. Maggie passes me
her tiny body. Cold and pale —
half my daughter's size at birth. Snorts
and screeches of sow's labor carry
in the wind this biting March dawn.

I wipe placenta from her snout, urge
this dying runt to life. Mother impulse:
I tuck her in my shirt, near my heart
wear her as she sleeps. Her cool skin
warms until it matches mine.

Maggie trims the tails and canine teeth
of every newborn   then counts:
Sixteen. Runt still alive?
I look beneath my jacket. When I rub
her bony chest, she stretches and whines.

All night, I cradle that pink-eared runt
feed her bottles of warmed cow's milk.
Coyotes yap and circle the ranch. We doze.
Across a moonless sky, a comet paints
trails of green and yellow light.

Acknowledgements

I thank wholeheartedly the editors who published earlier drafts of the following poems from this collection:

"Birthing Pigs in Kingman, Arizona" was a finalist for *Naugatuck River Review*, Winter 2010, Issue 7 — Contest Issue.

"Children's Park by London's Imperial War Museum" appeared in *Minerva Rising*, Issue 4, Fall 2013, Mothers.

"Cosmos," "Sophomore Year I Discovered Geometry," and "Corset Dream" appeared in *Minerva Rising*, Issue 10, 2016, The Body Issue.

"Cynthia Teaches Me How to Paint" was published September 1, 2014 in *Chest's* "Pectoriloquy," a poetry section in the journal of the American College of Chest Physicians, Volume 146, Issue 3.

"I Dream Wanda Plays Me Chopin" appeared in *Adanna*, Spring 2016, Women and Art.

"To the Woman on the Eastbound Midtown Direct" was a featured poem on *Minerva Rising Press,* a poetry website, on January 16, 2015.

"Mistress of Buttons and Keys" was posted as a *Soundcloud* recording on the website for Get Fresh Books, July 30, 2016.

Notes

The title of the poem, "The Cancer of Never Letting Go" is taken from a line in Jonathan Safran Foer's novel, *Extremely Loud and Incredibly Close.*

Kaisertown is the informal name given to a neighborhood in Buffalo near the Intersection of Clifton and South Ogden. Built on land sold from the Buffalo Creek Reservation by the Seneca Indians, it was originally populated by German immigrants in the mid-nineteenth century. The German influence on the neighborhood probably led to its nickname. In the 1890s, a significant influx of Polish immigrants led to the building of St. Casimir's church, where many of my relatives were baptized, married and buried. The church recently was closed except for special religious services for the remaining Polish-American community. My aunt Cecilia Grzybek's funeral in 2018 was one of those occasions.

My Heartfelt Gratitude

To my early mentors, poets Holly Scalera and Juliet Patterson, for early in-depth lessons in writing poetry.

To the late, brilliant Jane Mead for countering years of male-dominated indoctrination by introducing me to a world of women poets. To Michael Waters for building on that foundation, broadening my scope to include noted international poets; for his keen eye and ear, and for his valuable insights into my manuscript. To Ira Sadoff, who early on encouraged me to pursue my studies in poetry and whose wisdom about writing still guides me today. To Judith Vollmer, who taught me to trust my own voice, and who championed early drafts, as well as my final manuscript. Without the support and guidance of these four poets, I would have not completed *Fierce Geometry*.

To the Vermont College of Fine Arts for the manuscript workshop where I shaped this collection, and in particular, to Tina Chang whose insights and feedback provided valuable input. I also thank those who read my manuscript and offered feedback, particularly Cara Armstrong, Homa Zarghamee, Dan Piepenbring, and Soraya Salfaroosh Yahiaoui. Your suggestions, edits and support eased me through my final edits.

To my fellow poets at the Drew University Master of Fine Arts in Poetry, especially Lisa Alexander, Dario Beniquez, Jesse Burns, Rick Carter, David Crews, Fletch Fletcher, Brett Haymaker, Darla Himmeles, Ysabel Gonzalez, Peter Kirn, Bruce Lowry, Lynne McEniry, Yesenia Montilla, Sean Morrissey, Chelsea Palermo, Marisa Frasca Patinella, Sosha Pinson, and Heidi Sheridan. We grew together under the sun provided by Anne Marie Macari, Gerald Stern and Jean Valentine, and the community you collectively provided made me whole.

To Drew MFA mentor teacher-poets, particularly Aracelis Girmay, Joan Larkin, Anne Marie Macari, Mihaela Moscaliuc, Alicia Ostriker, Patrick Rosal, Ross Gay, Shara McCallum and Ellen Dore Watson for your inspiration and encouragement during my residency workshops.

Special thanks to Roberto Carlos Garcia, my friend, my fellow poet, and also my advisor throughout this entire publishing process. I am deeply grateful for your knowledge, support and encouragement. You made this dream a reality.

Friends Galina Bakhtiarova, Robin Patton, Alice Cahn, Ann Caroll, Laura Walthall, David Keller and Julie Meyers were my cheerleaders. Robin and Alice provided a safe space for writing getaways at their home in the North Fork. Robin, thanks for the bourbon and chocolates.

To my Buffalo family, whose shared heritage, experiences and love fueled my work in many ways. Special gratitude to my late aunt, Cindy Czapla, who lived an artist's life when it seemed beyond the reach of working class families. She mentored me in the art of creativity. To her son Ronald Czapla, whose sense of wonder and love of family are generous gifts to all of us who know him.

To my mother Deanna D'Andrea Fortkort who taught me that art mattered. To my father Thomas Fortkort who taught me that to be Irish was to revere poets and poetry. To my father-in-law Patrick Brancaccio who read my work over the years and encouraged me to keep on writing.

To my children, Nicholas, Madeleine and Anna Brancaccio, who gave me space to write and encouraged me to dream. Nick, thank you for teaching me to take criticism in stride. Maddy, thank you for teaching me how to take risks. Anna, thank you for teaching me to push through obstacles.

Most importantly, to David Brancaccio, my life partner, whose steadfast support makes my writing life possible. May all our whispered pillow dreams become realities.

CPSIA information can be obtained
at www.ICGtesting.com
Printed in the USA
JSHW022309250723
45385JS00003B/36